Original title:

Nature's Gentle Reminders

Copyright © 2024 Taago Leppik

All rights reserved.

Author: Augustus Flowman

ISBN HARDBACK: 978-9916-733-94-3

ISBN PAPERBACK: 978-9916-733-95-0

Bliss Found in Stillness

In quietude, the heart aligns,
Soft whispers echo through the pines.
The world fades into gentle hues,
As calm entwines in morning dew.

A breath, a pause, the moment grows,
Where nature's peace, so softly flows.
Amidst the trees, the shadows dance,
In stillness found, we find romance.

The river sings a tranquil tune,
Beneath the watchful gaze of moon.
With every ripple, love is shared,
In silent joy, our spirits bared.

In every leaf, in every breeze,
A sacred truth, a gentle ease.
In stillness lies a world so grand,
Where bliss awaits, if we but stand.

The Heartbeat of the Forest

Whispers echo through the trees,
Leaves dance softly in the breeze.
Sunlight filters through the green,
Nature's pulse, a rhythmic scene.

Birds take flight with joyous calls,
Rustling grass as silence falls.
Ferns unfurl, a gentle sigh,
Life awakens, brushes by.

Mushrooms peek from earth below,
Secrets in the shadows grow.
Streams babble tales of ages past,
In the forest, moments last.

Every heartbeat tells a tale,
In the woods, the spirits sail.
Harmony in every sound,
In this heart, life's beauty found.

Quiet Moments at Dusk

Twilight drapes the world in blue,
Stars awaken, one by one, too.
Whispers of the night arise,
Softly glowing, moonlit skies.

Crickets sing their evening song,
While shadows stretch, the night feels long.
Time pauses in a hushed embrace,
A tranquil peace, a sacred space.

The air is cool, a gentle sigh,
As dreams begin to float and fly.
Lost in thoughts that softly creep,
In quiet moments, worlds we keep.

Fading light, a day's farewell,
In stillness, deeper stories dwell.
Hold this calm, let worries fade,
In dusk's arms, the fears are laid.

The Caress of Dewdrops

Morning whispers soft and clear,
As dewdrops dance without a fear.
Light glimmers on each tender leaf,
Nature's gem, beyond belief.

Gentle hands of dawn align,
Kissing petals, bright and fine.
Each drop holds a sunlit dream,
A fleeting joy, a silver beam.

In stillness lies a sacred hush,
While flowers bloom in vibrant flush.
The earth awakens, life reborn,
Through every dewy morning's adorn.

As shadows linger, soft and light,
The world absorbs the dawn's delight.
In every drop, a tale retold,
Of nature's grace, forever bold.

A Symphony of Blossoms

In gardens vast, where colors play,
Nature sings in a grand ballet.
Petals swirl like notes in air,
A fragrant tune beyond compare.

Lilies dance in purest white,
While roses blush in morning light.
Daffodils nod with sunny grace,
In this most beautiful embrace.

Bees hum softly, drawn to feast,
On nectar sweet, a treasure beast.
Their melody, a buzzing charm,
In harmony, they weave no harm.

As twilight falls, the blooms still sing,
To the moonlight, their voices cling.
A night that wraps the day's delight,
In nature's arms, all feels right.

A Tapestry of Seasons

In bloom of spring, the flowers sing,
Their colors bright, a joyful thing.
The gentle breeze, a soft caress,
Awakens life, in nature's dress.

Summer sun, with golden rays,
Laughter echoes through warm days.
Fields of green, alive with cheer,
Time slows down, perfection near.

Autumn leaves in fiery dance,
Whisper secrets, take their chance.
Crisp air calls for coats and tea,
A tapestry of warmth for me.

Winter wraps in blankets white,
Stars emerge on velvet night.
With every flake, a tale is spun,
A cycle's end, and yet begun.

The Solace of Pebbles

On quiet shores where waters greet,
Pebbles lie beneath my feet.
Each one tells a tale of time,
Worn and smooth, a silent rhyme.

They glimmer softly in the light,
Reflecting dreams that take to flight.
Gathered here, a gentle throng,
Nature's chorus, sweet and strong.

Each step I take, the world unfolds,
In quiet whispers, secrets told.
Beneath the sky, so vast and free,
I find my peace, just me and me.

With every wave, the pebbles shift,
Nature's hands, the perfect gift.
In solitude, my heart can rest,
Among the stones, I feel so blessed.

The Dance of Shadows

In twilight's grip, the shadows play,
They stretch and bend, then fade away.
Whispers twirl upon the breeze,
In silent halls, with painted trees.

Moonlight washes soft and bright,
Illuminates the shivering night.
Figures move in gentle sway,
As darkness claims the end of day.

Beneath the stars, a secret song,
The dance goes on, both sweet and long.
In every corner, tales are spun,
Of dusk and dawn, of lost and won.

Each flicker tells a tale untold,
Of hearts entwined and dreams of old.
The shadows weave, a tapestry,
In the quietude, we find the key.

Celebrating the Quiet

In stillness lies a world so grand,
Where silence speaks, and whispers stand.
The gentle hush of falling leaves,
In quiet moments, the heart believes.

Beneath the sky, so vast and clear,
The calm invites the thoughts to steer.
With every breath, the spirit sighs,
In peaceful realms, the spirit flies.

The morning light brings dawn's embrace,
In warmth we find a sacred space.
As echoes fade and time slows down,
We wear the quiet like a crown.

So let us pause, and breathe it in,
In tranquil times, new dreams begin.
Embrace the still, and let it flow,
For in the quiet, we come to know.

The Language of the Petals

In the garden, whispers bloom,
Colors sing in soft perfume.
Each petal holds a tale of grace,
Dancing lightly in their place.

Breezes carry secrets sweet,
Nature's chorus, soft and fleet.
Stories etched in every hue,
Tales of love and skies so blue.

Bees and butterflies unite,
In a canvas, pure delight.
Every shade, a song declared,
In the quiet, hearts are bared.

Nature speaks in vibrant tones,
In the blooms, our truth is sown.
Listen close, the petals plea,
For in silence, joy's decree.

Gentle Hands of the Rain

Softly drumming on the leaves,
A lullaby the world receives.
Whispers in the cool, moist air,
Nature's touch, beyond compare.

Each droplet tells a story clear,
Washing woes and soothing fear.
Earth awakens, fresh and bright,
Underneath the gray, pure light.

Puddles form like mirrors wide,
Reflecting dreams we cannot hide.
Children splash and laughter rings,
In each drop, a world it brings.

The gentle hands embrace the ground,
In their grip, life's pulse is found.
With every fall, a promise stays,
In the rain, our hearts will blaze.

Footsteps in Forgotten Woods

In the hush of the twilight glow,
Footsteps wander where wildflowers grow.
Shadows dance as the sun sinks low,
Secrets whisper from below.

Ancient trees stretch their weary limbs,
Guarding tales in the light that dims.
Nature sings while the daylight swims,
A symphony of life begins.

Mossy carpets beneath our feet,
A gentle pull where pathways meet.
Echoes linger, soft and sweet,
In this haven, our hearts repeat.

Lost in dreams and the woodland's grace,
Every shadow finds its place.
In the silence, time's slow chase,
We find joy in nature's embrace.

The Breath of a Gentle Breeze

Whispers float on a twilight sigh,
Carrying secrets from the sky.
Dancing leaves in a blissful spree,
The heart of the world sings free.

Petals flutter in soft delight,
Caressed gently by the night.
Stars awaken, their glow so bright,
In harmony with the moon's light.

A breeze beckons, calling near,
Filling souls with tranquil cheer.
Promises linger in the atmosphere,
Where warmth and solace reappear.

With every puff, our spirits rise,
A lullaby of nature's sighs.
In the arms of the night, we devise,
Dreams that dance between the skies.

The Colors of Anticipation

Shades of red kiss the sky,
Golden hues begin to rise.
Whispers of dreams linger near,
Hope dances, shining bright.

In the morning's gentle glow,
Soft pastels paint the air.
Promises bloom with each breath,
Serenity waits with care.

Emerald fields sway with grace,
Azure whispers beckon near.
All the colors blend and twine,
Anticipation's song sincere.

As the twilight paints its cloak,
Indigo deepens the night.
Stars shimmer in quiet awe,
Glimmers of dreams take flight.

Melodies of a Midnight Breeze

A quiet hush drapes the night,
Moonlight spills soft on the ground.
Whispers carried on the air,
Nature's song a gentle sound.

Leaves rustle with secret tales,
Each note dances, sweet and low.
Stars twinkle as if in tune,
Melodies of dreams do flow.

Heartbeats sync with midnight's pulse,
The world sleeps in a soft dream.
Every breeze hums a soft song,
Life flows like a flowing stream.

Together, lost in the night,
Time stands still as shadows blend.
In the darkness, music thrives,
A serenade that won't end.

Lullabies from the River

Gentle whispers in the breeze,
The river sings beneath the trees.
Moonlight dances on the shore,
Lullabies that soothe and soar.

Rippling currents, soft and low,
Carrying tales of long ago.
Birds serenade the night with grace,
In this tranquil, sacred space.

Stars reflect on waters deep,
As nature wraps its arms to keep.
Flowing dreams in silver light,
Cradled softly through the night.

Let the river's song embrace,
As we drift in time and space.
Tranquil hearts and minds set free,
In harmony with all we see.

Reflections on Still Waters

In the mirror of the lake,
Silent secrets softly wake.
Clouds unfold their gentle sigh,
As sunlight dances from the sky.

Ripples break the perfect glass,
Time halts and moments pass.
Nature whispers, dreams ignite,
In the calmness of the night.

Trees bow down to greet the stream,
While shadows weave a quiet dream.
The world feels still, the heart is light,
As stars emerge to share their light.

In reflections, we find our place,
Embraced by nature's warm embrace.
Breathe in deep, let worries fade,
In this peace, our souls are laid.

The Weaving of Seasons Past

In the quiet woods the whispers play,
Leaves of amber dance and sway,
Echoes of laughter weave through the air,
Memories linger, woven with care.

Winter's breath cools the weary ground,
Silent blankets lie all around,
Embers fade in the twilight glow,
Stories hidden, only time knows.

Spring emerges with a soft embrace,
Colors burst in a delicate race,
Petals unfold, a vibrant display,
Life is reborn in a beautiful way.

Summer's warmth calls forth the sun,
Life's bright songs, laughter and fun,
In golden fields where children run,
The weaving of seasons has just begun.

Where Silence Meets Serenity

In the stillness of early dawn,
Misty whispers gently drawn,
Nature breathes, a soft refrain,
Where silence cradles peace like rain.

Mountains stand in solemn grace,
Their shadows touch the tranquil place,
A quiet stream flows smooth and clear,
Each drop a note, a prayer sincere.

Beneath the stars, the night unfolds,
Stories of dreams and secrets told,
In hushed tones, the world seems to rest,
Where silence gathers, hearts feel blessed.

With every breath, the calm descends,
In silence, the universe bends,
Serenity blooms, a fragrant art,
Whispering softly to each heart.

The Embrace of Evening Mist

As day departs, the shadows creep,
Whispers of night in silence keep.
The world enfolded, soft and grey,
In twilight's arms, we lose our way.

In dusky hues, the trees now stand,
Veils of fog caress the land.
The stars awaken, shy and bright,
As dreams unfurl, in velvet night.

Night's gentle kiss upon the stream,
Reflects the moon's silver beam.
With every sigh, the darkness breathes,
A secret kept 'neath swaying leaves.

In this embrace, we find our peace,
As worries fade and troubles cease.
The evening mist, a tender hug,
Wraps the world, warm and snug.

Murmurs of the Ocean Shore

The tide recedes, a gentle sigh,
Whispers mingle, low and high.
Waves caress the golden sand,
An endless dance, a timeless band.

Seagulls cry with joyful glee,
Chasing breezes wild and free.
The salty air, a lover's touch,
Embracing all with tender hush.

Shells lie scattered, stories told,
Of sunlit days and nights so bold.
Footprints fade, the water swells,
Each frothy wave, a tale it tells.

The horizon blushes, paints the sky,
As day retreats, the stars comply.
In ocean's song, our hearts align,
Forever lost in love divine.

Breezes that Speak

Whispers of wind dance through the trees,
Carrying tales from far-off seas.
Gentle caresses, soft and light,
They weave a magic in the night.

Leaves flutter softly with each sigh,
As dreams take flight beneath the sky.
Nature's breath, a sweet refrain,
Sings of joy and hints of pain.

In the stillness, listen well,
For breezes hold the stories they tell.
A symphony of life unfolds,
In whispers soft, the truth it holds.

So let your heart be open wide,
Embrace the whispers, let them guide.
For in the breeze, we find our peace,
In every sigh, our cares can cease.

The Call of Distant Mountains

Silent sentinels stand tall and proud,
In the distance, draped in clouds.
Their whispers echo through the vale,
Telling tales of storms and hail.

Paths that wander through the pines,
Lead to peaks where sunlight shines.
A call from heights where eagles soar,
Inviting souls to seek for more.

With every step, the heart will race,
In the embrace of nature's grace.
Mountains beckon, strong and true,
Promising horizons new.

So heed the call, let spirits climb,
To places untouched by time.
For in the mountains, we are free,
In their shadows, our souls can be.

The Warmth of a Sunlit Meadow

Golden rays dance on the ground,
While whispers of breezes swirl around.
Flowers bloom in vibrant cheer,
Nature's beauty, bright and clear.

Beneath the sky, the world does gleam,
A place where hearts can softly dream.
Gentle hills cradle the light,
Peaceful moments, pure delight.

Birds sing sweetly from up high,
Their melodies, a joyful sigh.
The scent of grass fills the air,
A tranquil charm beyond compare.

As day unfolds, the shadows play,
In this haven, I long to stay.
Wrapped in warmth, lost in time,
The meadow sings a perfect rhyme.

Fleeting Moments of Awe

A sunrise spills its golden hues,
A canvas fresh with vibrant views.
Each second fleeting, yet divine,
In whispered winds, we intertwine.

A child's laugh, a gentle breeze,
Time seems to pause, just to please.
In every glance, a spark ignites,
Capturing joy in tiny bites.

The first snowflakes, a silken kiss,
Moments like these, we can't dismiss.
Nature's wonders, quick to fade,
Yet in our hearts, they are replayed.

Under starlit skies we stand,
Grasping the mysteries at hand.
Fleeting yet, so deep and wide,
In awe, we let our hearts reside.

Gentle Touch of Morning Dew

Upon the grass, a shimmer bright,
A tender kiss from night to light.
Each droplet lingers, soft and clear,
Whispers of dawn, so fresh, so near.

The flowers wake, their petals sigh,
Embraced by warmth, they reach for the sky.
In stillness' grace, the world renews,
With every glance, I'm lost in hues.

A breeze awakens, sweet and light,
Carrying scents of pure delight.
Nature's symphony, a soft refrain,
In gentle touch, no hint of pain.

As shadows fade, the day begins,
With tender moments, life quietly spins.
In morning's glow, my heart takes flight,
Embraced by love, a tranquil sight.

Sunbeams Through the Canopy

Golden rays cut through the trees,
Dancing light upon the breeze.
Whispers of warmth in emerald shade,
Nature's canvas, a bright parade.

Leaves shimmer bright, a jeweled crown,
As sunbeams chase the gloom around.
Their laughter echoes, soft and sweet,
A melody where heartbeats meet.

Birds in flight, on shadows play,
Writing stories in their ballet.
A fleeting glimpse of joy and cheer,
Moments held, forever dear.

Through branches woven, light cascades,
A tapestry where beauty fades.
In this embrace of sun and tree,
I find my place, forever free.

The Heartbeat of the River

Beneath the willow, waters flow,
Whispers of secrets, ancient and slow.
Each ripple carries a story untold,
In the heart of the river, treasures unfold.

Silent reflections on the glassy sheen,
Nature's pulse beats, steady and keen.
The fish dart swiftly, a flash of green,
In the rhythm of water, life's serene.

Pebbles hum softly, cradled by tide,
Beneath the surface, where dreams abide.
The heartbeat echoes, in tune with the night,
Guiding the lost with soft, glowing light.

The river beckons, a call to embrace,
Whispers of peace, in a calming space.
A melody timeless, forever will play,
In the heart of the river, we drift and sway.

Shadows Dancing with the Sky

As daylight fades, the shadows rise,
Ballet of dusk under twilight skies.
Figures entwined in a graceful flight,
Painted in colors of fading light.

The moon peeks out, a sentinel bright,
Guiding the dancers through the night.
On whispers of wind, they twirl and spin,
In a waltz with the stars, where dreams begin.

Every flicker tells a tale of old,
A story of warmth as the night unfolds.
With each gentle murmur, they sway and bend,
In the quiet embrace where the world can mend.

Together they sway, shadows in play,
Painting the night, melting worries away.
In this dance of magic, we find our way,
Under the canopy where dreams hold sway.

Harmony in the Rustling Grass

In fields where whispers dance and sway,
The grass sings soft, in gentle play.
A symphony of nature's song,
Where all belong, where hearts grow strong.

The breeze caresses, a tender touch,
Each blade a note, it means so much.
Underneath the vast blue sky,
The world feels right, the spirits fly.

A harmony found in every hue,
In shades of green, in morning dew.
Life pulses on, a beautiful quest,
In rustling grass, we find our rest.

Together we dance, as shadows cast,
In the embrace of time so vast.
Nature's rhythm, a sacred trust,
In every moment, in every gust.

Secrets of the Moonlit Night

Beneath the glow of silver light,
Whispers float on softest night.
Stars twinkle secrets from afar,
As dreams are born in night's bazaar.

The shadows linger, tales untold,
In the deep dark, mysteries unfold.
Each breath of night, a promise made,
In moonlight's embrace, fears start to fade.

Gentle night sighs with ancient grace,
In this stillness, we find our place.
With eyes closed tight, we feel the glow,
Secrets shared where moonbeams flow.

In every heartbeat, in every sigh,
The night reveals what we deny.
So let us wander, lost in delight,
And treasure the secrets of the night.

The Tranquil Call of Birds

In morning light, the robins sing,
A sweet refrain, the day might bring.
Above the trees, a soft breeze flows,
As nature wakes from silent doze.

With flutters bright, the sparrows play,
In harmony, they greet the day.
Each note a thread, a lovely weave,
In songs that soothe, we dare believe.

Through rustling leaves, their whispers glide,
A serenade, the world's warm guide.
In every chirp and gentle call,
We find our peace, we feel it all.

As twilight drapes its velvet shroud,
The echo fades, yet still so loud.
In hearts of those who pause to hear,
The tranquil call draws ever near.

Elegy of the Expanding Sky

Beneath vast realms, where whispers roam,
The sky unfolds its endless dome.
In hues of dusk, the stars appear,
A silent grace, they draw us near.

Lost moments drift like clouds above,
In the canvas, we learn to love.
Each gasp of wind, a fleeting sigh,
An elegy of dreams gone by.

The sun retreats, with colors bold,
While night unveils its tales of old.
In every change, a story told,
An expanding sky, forever gold.

As constellations start their dance,
In whispered lore, we take a chance.
To dream anew, beneath the vast,
An elegy that holds the past.

Nature's Subtle Tapestry

In twilight's glow, the shadows play,
Leaves dance gently, they sway and sway.
Colors blend on the canvas wide,
Nature's art, her graceful pride.

Mountains rise, their peaks adorned,
With snowflakes bright, the world reborn.
Rivers weave with a silver thread,
Guiding dreams where the soft winds spread.

Whispers of flowers in the breeze,
Their sweet perfume, a soft tease.
Each petal tells a tale untold,
In hues of crimson, yellow, gold.

Beneath the stars, the night's embrace,
Moonlit paths, a tranquil space.
Nature's breath, so calm, so pure,
In every heartbeat, peace we secure.

The Solace of Whispering Pines

In forests deep where silence reigns,
Whispering pines dispel our pains.
With gentle arms, they reach for skies,
Guardians bold, where solace lies.

The rustling needles sing a tune,
Underneath the watchful moon.
Soft echoed calls, the wind's caress,
Nature's hymn, a sweet distress.

Dappled light on the forest floor,
Opens paths, reveals the lore.
With every step, our spirits soar,
In pines' embrace, we find much more.

As twilight falls, the shadows blend,
A tranquil night where hearts can mend.
Beneath the stars, in dreams we pine,
We find our peace, the woods divine.

The Pulse of a Waiting Valley

In the hush of dawn's first light,
The valley breathes, so still, so bright.
Mountains watch, their shadows cast,
Whispers of the night, now past.

A river flows, its song so clear,
Carrying dreams, both far and near.
Trees stand tall, their leaves a dance,
Cradling secrets in nature's trance.

Beneath the soil, life stirs awake,
Wonders hidden, the ground does make.
Insects hum, a chorus true,
Each heartbeat pulls the morning through.

The sun ascends, painting skies bright,
Chasing away the remnants of night.
The pulse of life, it beats in time,
In this waiting valley, pure and sublime.

Glistening Trails of Ants

On the warm earth, a path unfolds,
Glistening trails, a story told.
Tiny workers march in line,
Carrying seeds, their labor divine.

Through blades of grass, they weave and roam,
Each little ant, far from home.
In the sun, their bodies gleam,
A tapestry of nature's dream.

Underneath the vast blue sky,
They scurry fast, they wander by.
On this quest for food and grain,
In the bustling world, they remain.

A kingdom built on strength and will,
Silent stories, a hunger to fill.
With glistening trails that never cease,
Ants dance the dance of life and peace.

A Canvas of Starlit Dreams

Under the veil of night's embrace,
Stars weave tales in silent grace.
Whispers of hope in the cool air,
Painting dreams that linger there.

Each twinkle holds a secret bright,
Guiding hearts through the endless night.
Moonlight dances on silver streams,
Awakening the world of dreams.

Softly the shadows cast their spell,
In the quiet where wishes dwell.
A canvas drawn in cosmic beams,
A journey born from starlit dreams.

So let your spirit drift and soar,
In the magic of evermore.
For in the skies, our hopes ignite,
A canvas painted by the night.

The Sway of the Tall Grasses

In fields where gentle breezes play,
Tall grasses sway in a rhythmic way.
Whispers of nature, soft and sweet,
Dancing slowly to a heart's beat.

Beneath the sun, they bend and sway,
Holding secrets of the day.
Each blade a story, a tale untold,
In hues of green, in shades of gold.

Natures' laughter fills the air,
The tall grasses sway without a care.
With every gust, they rise and fall,
A harmonious dance, embracing all.

As twilight sets and shadows grow,
The grasses whisper, soft and low.
A tranquil balm, a soothing flow,
In the sway of the tall grasses' show.

Sketches of a Dusk

The sun dips slow, a brush of gold,
Clouds gather softly, stories told.
Shadows stretch long, the world at peace,
In the twilight, all worries cease.

Birds take flight, painting the air,
Whispers of night, a gentle prayer.
Stars peek through the curtain of blue,
In this moment, everything feels new.

The breeze carries scents of the day,
As colors fade, they softly sway.
A canvas of dreams, the night unfolds,
In every hue, a secret holds.

Echoes of laughter linger near,
In the dusk, we shed every fear.
With each stroke, the dusk we frame,
In this sketch, we find our names.

The Art of Blooming

In a garden where silence plays,
Petals unfurl in sunlit rays.
Colors burst forth, a vibrant song,
Nature whispers where we belong.

Dewdrops glisten on emerald leaves,
The dance of life, the heart believes.
In gentle winds, seeds take flight,
Painting the world in pure delight.

Every bud holds a timeless dream,
Unfolding softly, a radiant beam.
In love's embrace, we find our way,
The art of blooming day by day.

In twilight's glow, we're never apart,
Each blossom whispers life to the heart.
With every breath, new stories start,
In the garden, we play our part.

Echoes of the Forest Floor

Beneath the trees, where shadows play,
Whispers of leaves dance and sway.
A carpet of moss, soft and green,
Nature's stillness, serene yet keen.

Sunbeams peek through branches high,
Chasing the dreams that linger nigh.
Footsteps echo on the ground,
Secrets of the wild abound.

Birds sing sweetly, a chorus bright,
Filling the air with pure delight.
A rustle here, a call from far,
Every sound, a guiding star.

In the heart of this tranquil space,
Time slows down, a gentle grace.
Echoes of life, both near and far,
In the forest's arms, we are never ajar.

A Symphony of Seasons

Spring awakens with colors bold,
Petals unfold, a story told.
Bees buzz low, a sweet refrain,
Life returns to the earth again.

Summer's warmth envelops tight,
Days stretch long, hearts feel light.
Whispers of waves on sandy shores,
A vibrant dance that nature pours.

Autumn's cloak in amber hues,
Leaves fall gently, a golden muse.
Crisp and cool, the air ignites,
Harvest moons and cozy nights.

Winter drapes the world in white,
Silent landscapes, pure delight.
Fires crackle, stories unfold,
A tapestry of life, rich and bold.

Serenity Beneath the Stars

In the hush of night so deep,
Stars above begin to weep,
Whispers of the winds that sigh,
Dreams awakened, soaring high.

Moonlight dances on the lake,
Gentle ripples softly break,
Nature's breath in stillness reigns,
A tranquil heart, and peace remains.

Constellations tell their tale,
Guiding souls on night's soft sail,
In this realm where silence speaks,
Serenity the spirit seeks.

Wrapped in shadows, hope ignites,
Cloaked in comfort, stars are sights,
A celestial embrace so rare,
In this moment, beyond compare.

Embrace of the Morning Mist

The dawn awakens with a kiss,
Morning mist in gentle bliss,
Veiling trees and fields so wide,
Nature's pulse where dreams abide.

Sunlight breaks and colors blend,
A canvas new, the day will tend,
Whispers soft, the breeze will weave,
In this moment, hearts believe.

Birds in flight on wings of grace,
Chasing shadows, leaving trace,
In the mist, the world feels whole,
As the sun ignites the soul.

Embrace the day with open arms,
Feel its warmth, its tender charms,
In the glow of morning's light,
Hope is born, dispelling night.

The Breath of the Earth

Whispers dance upon the breeze,
Nature sings beneath the trees.
Colors bloom in vibrant span,
Life unfolds across the land.

Mountains hold the sun's first glow,
Rivers weave the tales they know.
Sky and earth in harmony,
Echoes of eternity.

In the meadow, shadows play,
Rays of gold in bright array.
Gentle hands of time caress,
Every moment a soft bless.

Beneath the stars, the world sighs,
In its heart, the secret lies.
Every heartbeat, every sigh,
Breathes the earth, we live, we die.

The Souvenir of a Starlit Night

Underneath a silver sky,
Dreamers watch the shadows fly.
Whispers of a soft embrace,
Every star, a fleeting trace.

Moonlight drapes the tranquil sea,
Glistening like a memory.
Waves cascade with gentle grace,
Cradling dreams in their embrace.

Moments captured in the dark,
Fleeting hopes, a fragile spark.
In the quiet, hearts align,
Souvenirs of love divine.

Starlit paths that lead us home,
In the night, we're not alone.
Each soft glow, a tale is spun,
In the dark, we've just begun.

Under the Canopy of Stars

Beneath the dome of night, we lay,
Whispers dance in silver light,
The moon, a guardian so bright,
Dreams unfold in soft array.

The world feels small, the sky so wide,
Constellations tell their tales,
With every twinkle, love prevails,
In this warmth, we'll bide our time.

Crickets chirp a gentle tune,
As shadows linger, hearts entwine,
Each sigh, a secret divine,
Underneath the watchful moon.

Stars above, our silent friends,
They guide us through the cosmic sea,
In this moment, you and me,
A bond that time will never bends.

The Drift of Autumn Leaves

Leaves descend in shades of gold,
Whispers of the chilling air,
Nature's brush, a tale retold,
As summer's warmth begins to share.

The trees stand tall, a canvas bare,
Rustling tales of days gone by,
The wind, it sings a lover's sigh,
In every swirl, there's beauty rare.

Patches of crimson dance along,
Swaying gently to nature's tune,
A fleeting glimpse, a sweet monsoon,
In the breeze, I hear our song.

With every step, a crunching sound,
Memories of seasons past,
In Fall's embrace, we hold steadfast,
As golden dreams weave all around.

The Unseen Thread of Life

In shadows soft, where secrets dwell,
A whispering truth no words can tell.
We weave our dreams on fragile lace,
An unseen thread in time and space.

Moments dance like fireflies bright,
Guiding us through the velvet night.
Each heartbeat sings, a silent song,
Binding us where we all belong.

With every twist, the story grows,
Like rivers flow, as life bestows.
In silent prayers, we reach above,
Connected still by threads of love.

So walk with grace on paths unknown,
For in each step, we're never alone.
Together we rise, together we thrive,
Embracing the unseen thread of life.

Echoes of Earth's Embrace

Beneath the sky, where wildflowers sway,
Nature sings in a timeless ballet.
Mountains stand tall, guardians old,
Their stories whispered, their secrets told.

The rivers hum a soothing tune,
A lullaby bathed in the light of the moon.
Waves cradle shores with a tender kiss,
In the heart of the earth, we find our bliss.

Birds take flight on the breath of the breeze,
Painting the air with effortless ease.
In every rustle, a language pure,
Echoes of life, both wild and sure.

So let us wander, hand in hand,
Through forests deep and golden sand.
In each embrace, our spirits trace,
The echoes of earth's warm embrace.

Shadows of an Ancient Tree

Beneath the boughs, the whispers play,
Ancient secrets that sway and lay.
Time drips slowly, like dew at dawn,
A sentinel quiet, through ages drawn.

Roots entwined in stories deep,
Guarding the dreams that nature keeps.
In its shade, a world unfolds,
With every rustle, a tale retold.

Leaves of green in endless dance,
Casting shadows, a fleeting glance.
Echoes linger, a soft embrace,
Life weaves softly in this sacred space.

Yet seasons change, and winds do sigh,
The ancient tree watches time pass by.
In twilight's glow, a farewell call,
Its heart beats strong, through rise and fall.

Murmurs of the Meadow

In the meadow where flowers bloom,
Soft whispers carried in the loom.
Grass sways gently to nature's tune,
Beneath the watchful gaze of the moon.

Bees are buzzing, a lively song,
Dancing amidst where they belong.
Colors bright in morning light,
All are welcome, no end in sight.

A brook nearby sings crystal clear,
With each ripple, secrets appear.
Nature's rhythm, a gentle flow,
In the meadow, serenity grows.

As the sun dips low in the sky,
The shadows stretch, and crickets sigh.
Night blankets softly, dreams take wing,
In the meadow, life's whispers ring.

Soft Echoes of the Stream

Whispers dance upon the brook,
A gentle sigh, a quiet look.
Pebbles glint in dappled light,
Soft echoes call throughout the night.

Willows sway, their branches low,
Crickets sing, the shadows grow.
Ripples weave a tale so sweet,
Nature's song, a soft heartbeat.

Misty veils on morning's breath,
Life awakens, conquers death.
Bubble laughter, clear and bright,
Water's dream in purest sight.

In this realm where peace abides,
Every thought in stillness hides.
Soft echoes blend with time's own gleam,
Forever held in nature's dream.

When the Sunrise Smiles

Morning breaks with hues of gold,
A canvas bright, a tale retold.
Birds rejoice, their songs in flight,
When the sunrise smiles so bright.

Clouds blush softly, kissed by light,
Dewdrops glisten, pure delight.
Every shadow finds its grace,
In the warmth of this embrace.

Fields awake in colors bold,
Stories gather, yet untold.
As the day begins to climb,
Every moment feels like rhyme.

Hope arises with the dawn,
New beginnings, dreams reborn.
So let your heart take wing and soar,
When the sunrise smiles, explore.

Conversations with the Seasons

Spring whispers soft, with blossoms in bloom,
Winter replies, in a quiet, white room.
Summer chuckles, as daylight extends,
Autumn nods wisely, as daylight descends.

Winter's chill bites, a crisp, cold embrace,
Spring makes a promise, to quicken the pace.
Summer's warmth glows, a fiery delight,
Autumn brings harvest, in golden sunlight.

Spring dances lightly, on petals so bright,
Winter's stillness holds, the stars of the night.
Summer's laughter echoes, through trees of green,
Autumn's deep whispers, in hues so serene.

The seasons engage, in a timeless ballet,
Each plays a part, as night turns to day.
Together they weave, a tapestry grand,
In conversations that span, all the land.

The Alchemy of Rain and Sun

Rain drips softly, a gentle caress,
Sunbeam's response, in warmth it profess.
Together they paint, the world in a glow,
In droplets and light, life finds a flow.

Clouds gather whispers, of stories untold,
While sunlight breaks through, in ribbons of gold.
Each droplet that falls, is a note in the air,
Each ray of the sun, is a spark of the fair.

Rain dances freely, on rooftops and leaves,
Sun wraps around, where the heart believes.
Together they blend, in a symphony sweet,
Creating a rhythm, where earth and sky meet.

The alchemy blooms, in gardens anew,
With rain as a lover, and sun as a view.
Nature's great magic, in cycles it spins,
A heart full of joy, when the rain gently wins.

The Scent of Earth After Rain

The clouds have wept, the earth now sighs,
Fresh scents arise where mud complies.
Leaves glisten bright in gentle glow,
Nature inhales, reviving slow.

Puddles form where sun's light fades,
Reflections dance in soft cascades.
The air is rich, a fragrant balm,
Each droplet whispers, calm and calm.

From deep brown soil to vibrant green,
The world reborn, fresh and serene.
A symphony of scents unfurls,
A message pure from ancient swirls.

So let me breathe this moment near,
In every drop, the earth's sweet cheer.
The scent of life, pure as a brand,
A treasure held in nature's hand.

The Brush of a Butterfly's Wing

In the garden's soft embrace,
A butterfly takes flight with grace.
Its colors burst, a fleeting show,
On petals bright, it dips, and flows.

With gentle touch, it stirs the bloom,
A waltz of life, dispelling gloom.
A whisper light in summer's day,
A brush of wings that dance and sway.

It flits through air, on currents high,
Painting joy beneath the sky.
With every flap, a tale is spun,
Of fragile beauty, life begun.

Catch this moment, hold it tight,
The brush of wings, a pure delight.
In nature's realm, where wonders cling,
We've caught the grace of a butterfly's wing.

Whispers of the Wind

In twilight's hush, the breezes sigh,
Soft secrets float as clouds drift by.
Through trees they weave, a gentle song,
Nature's voice where all belong.

A dance of leaves, a rustling tune,
The wind's soft breath beneath the moon.
It carries tales of far-off lands,
Stirring dreams with unseen hands.

Whispers curl 'round the mountain peaks,
In every corner, the silence speaks.
With every gust, a story spins,
In every pause, a world begins.

Embrace the night, let shadows blend,
With every whisper, let hearts mend.
For in the wind, we find the trace,
Of love and loss, of time and space.

The Soft Caress of Dawn

As night retreats, the sky ignites,
A palette spread of warm delights.
The stars dissolve, the shadows fade,
In morning's light, new dreams are laid.

The soft caress of golden rays,
Awakens hope in countless ways.
Birds begin their cheerful songs,
As daylight bursts and night belongs.

A whispered promise in the air,
Brushes our skin with tender care.
Each beam of light, a gentle nudge,
Inviting hearts to rise and judge.

The world transforms with every breath,
In dawn's embrace, we conquer death.
Let moments bloom like flowers born,
In the soft caress of every dawn.

The Subtle Art of Leaf Fall

In the gentle breeze they dance,
Colors blend in a fleeting glance,
Whispers of autumn fill the air,
Nature's canvas, beyond compare.

Golden hues and crimson bright,
A carpet forms under soft light,
Each leaf tells a story untold,
As seasons change, the new takes hold.

Fallen dreams on the ground lie,
Softly crunching as we pass by,
Memories swirl with every gust,
Turning to dust, as all things must.

Beneath the trees, a quiet space,
Reflecting time's gentle embrace,
The subtle art of letting go,
In leaf fall's dance, we find the flow.

Cradled by Clouds

Drifting softly through the sky,
Whispers of the winds go by,
Puffy forms in shades of white,
Cradling dreams like stars at night.

Sunlight kisses edges bright,
Creating shadows, pure delight,
Each cloud a story, drifting free,
Together in this tapestry.

Riding high without a care,
In the quiet, time laid bare,
Cotton castles loom ahead,
A world of wonder, gently spread.

Beneath their shade, the earth sighs,
As raindrops dance from painted skies,
Cradled by clouds, we find our way,
In soft embrace, forever stay.

Petals Fall Like Secrets

Petals drift on whispered winds,
Thoughts concealed in soft descent.
Nature's tales, on breezes penned,
Moments lost, yet ever spent.

Colors fade, yet dreams remain,
Silent stories, softly told.
In the garden, joy and pain,
Memories in hues of gold.

Underneath the twilight sky,
Shadows dance, the secrets sigh.
Songs of love, of loss, of time,
In the stillness, echoes chime.

Softly now, the night descends,
Petals fall like liquid stars.
In the dark, the heart amends,
Finding peace amidst the scars.

The Language of Leaves

Leaves converse with gentle sighs,
Rustling speaks of ancient lore.
In the silence, wisdom lies,
Nature's voice, a soft encore.

Green whispers float on the breeze,
Each a word, a soothing balm.
Branches sway with perfect ease,
Underneath, a hidden calm.

Every turn, a new refrain,
Nature's symphony unfolds.
Sunlit moments, soft and plain,
Stories in the air retold.

Seasons shift, the colors change,
Leaves embrace a fleeting dance.
In their shade, lives rearrange,
Life's vast tale, a second chance.

In the twilight, shadows weave,
Nature's script in every shade.
With each fall, we learn to grieve,
Understanding in silence made.

The Gift of Change

In autumn's embrace, leaves fall down,
Whispers of change in a crisp brown gown.
The wind carries tales from far away,
Reminding us all, it's okay to sway.

With each dawn's light, the new day breaks,
Offering paths, a choice it makes.
Embrace the unknown, let fears subside,
For in every shift, new dreams abide.

Like rivers that twist, and mountains that rise,
Life dances onward beneath vast skies.
We shed our old skins, reveal the bright,
In the gift of change, we find our light.

So take a deep breath, let go of the past,
In the ever-flowing, make your heart vast.
For change is a gift, an artist's hand,
Crafting our journeys across life's land.

Beneath the Canopy of Time

Beneath the leaves, the whispers flow,
Stories of ages, both high and low.
Each branch above holds secrets untold,
In the shade of time, mysteries unfold.

Sunlight flickers through emerald shade,
Dancing with shadows, where dreams are laid.
With every tick, the moment's a friend,
Beneath the canopy, where pathways blend.

Roots intertwine, connecting the past,
In the embrace of time, love holds fast.
Listen closely, for time softly speaks,
In the quiet moments, wisdom peaks.

As seasons change, the cycles repeat,
Life harmonizes, both bitter and sweet.
Beneath the vast sky, in the light we seek,
In the canopy of time, our spirits peak.

In the Arms of the Earth

Beneath the sky, where shadows play,
The gentle ground holds me at bay.
With whispers soft, the grasses sway,
In nature's arms, I long to stay.

Mountains rise, embracing the sun,
Where rivers flow, their courses run.
The forest hums, a soothing song,
In earth's great arms, I feel so strong.

Petals fall, a fragrant rain,
Each breath I take, a sweet refrain.
In every hue, life starts anew,
In soil's embrace, I find what's true.

Stars emerge, the night takes hold,
Under the sky, stories unfold.
In twilight's grasp, the world stands still,
In the earth's arms, I find my will.

Reflections in a Still Pond

Glimmers dance on water's face,
A mirror holds the sky's embrace.
In silent depth, the world does wait,
For ripples soft, a quiet fate.

Leaves drift down on whispered breeze,
Each moment still, as time would freeze.
The pond reflects a tranquil scene,
Where thoughts are pure, and minds are keen.

Dragonflies flit, a fleeting grace,
In nature's calm, they find their place.
Beneath the surface, secrets lie,
In quiet depths, the heart's reply.

As stars gaze down, the night unfolds,
In water's arms, the story's told.
With each breath, I find release,
In reflections deep, I find my peace.

A Song for the Wandering Clouds

Drifting high in azure skies,
Softly whispered lullabies.
Chasing dreams with gentle grace,
They paint stories in their place.

Mighty storms and sunlit rays,
Changing hues in endless plays.
Floating free on winds so wild,
Nature's beauty, pure and mild.

Castles built in air so light,
Fleeting forms that fade from sight.
A tapestry of white and gray,
In the heavens, they sway and play.

Oh, how they roam, unfettered,
A dance of freedom, unmeasured.
In their journey, we partake,
A song of clouds, we softly make.

Smiles Hidden in the Grass

Beneath the blades, a secret lies,
Where daisies bloom and laughter flies.
A tapestry of green so bright,
Whispers of joy in morning light.

Crickets chirp a sweet refrain,
Nature's chorus, soft and plain.
In the shadows, small friends peek,
As sunbeams dance and flowers speak.

Tiny wonders, soft and small,
Painting smiles, enchanting all.
In every crevice, life abounds,
In simple places, love surrounds.

So bend down low, take time to see,
The hidden gems that wish to be.
For in the grass, life's magic glows,
With every smile that nature shows.

Nature's Own Love Poem

In the garden where flowers sway,
Bees hum softly, welcoming day.
Leaves whisper secrets to the breeze,
Nature sings love, putting hearts at ease.

Mountains rise, strong and tall,
Rivers dance, answering the call.
With every sunset, colors blend,
Nature's embrace, a timeless friend.

Stars twinkle in the night's warm glow,
Moonlight kisses the earth below.
In every rustle, a story unfolds,
Nature's own love, a beauty that holds.

With each sunrise, hope is reborn,
In every dawn, a fresh adorn.
Nature whispers, soft and low,
A love that's boundless, forever to grow.

Fragments of a Serene Sky

Clouds drift gently, soft and white,
Painting dreams in morning light.
A canvas vast, of blue and grey,
Whispers of peace in shades of play.

Gentle winds weave through the trees,
Voices carried on the breeze.
Sunbeams dance, and shadows sway,
Fragments of joy, in natural ballet.

Stars emerge as twilight descends,
Nighttime magic, where silence bends.
Constellations share their tales,
In this serene sky, wonder prevails.

Each dawn a promise, each dusk a sigh,
Moments captured, as time goes by.
Nature's beauty, forever nigh,
Fragments of a serene sky.

The Embrace of Rocky Shores

Waves crash hard on rugged stone,
Whispers of the sea's sweet moan.
Seagulls call in wild delight,
Nature's dance in fading light.

Tides that pull and tides that sway,
Echoes of a long-gone day.
Shells and seaweed, treasures found,
In this place, my heart is bound.

Cliffs rise high against the sky,
Where the seabirds soar and fly.
Salt-kissed air, the ocean's breath,
In this moment, find sweet depth.

Embrace the wild, the woven strands,
Life unfolds on shifting sands.
A symphony of earth and sea,
In rocky shores, I'm truly free.

Twilight's Quiet Promise

As twilight drapes the world in blue,
Stars awaken, one or two.
The sun dips low, a gentle sigh,
Whispers of night crawl the sky.

Moonlight spills on silver streams,
Weaving softly through my dreams.
In this hush, a tender thought,
Hope is found in shadows caught.

Silent moments, soft and sweet,
Where the day and night do meet.
Nature holds a breathless pause,
In the twilight, I find flaws.

Promises of dawn will wake,
Through the dark, the light will break.
Rest assured, the sun will rise,
With each night, a new surprise.

The Calm Before the Storm

The sky hangs low, a cloak of gray,
Whispers of wind in a hushed ballet.
Trees hold their breath, as shadows sway,
Nature awaits, in silence they stay.

Birds cease their song, the air feels thick,
A distant rumble, the clock ticks quick.
Clouds gather close, a brewing trick,
Tension builds up, a fate to pick.

Lightning flickers in the heavy air,
The world stands still, a moment rare.
Hearts race fast, as time we bear,
The storm will come, with little care.

And then, with fury, the heavens break,
Rain pours down, the earth will shake.
Yet in that tempest, we find our wake,
The calm returns, new beauty to make.

Melodies of the Meadowlark

In golden fields, where daisies dance,
A meadowlark sings, lost in a trance.
Each note is bright, a fleeting chance,
To capture joy, in nature's romance.

The sun dips low, painting skies ablaze,
As dusk approaches, the world's in a haze.
His lilting tune, a warm embrace,
Echoes softly, in twilight's grace.

With every chirp, a story unfolds,
Of summer days, and memories bold.
In the cool breeze, a tale retold,
Life's simple pleasures, a treasure to hold.

As night descends, the lark takes flight,
A final song, to end the light.
Yet in our hearts, the melody's bright,
A reminder sweet, of nature's delight.

Whispers of the Leaves

In the grove where shadows play,
The leaves converse in soft ballet.
A rustling sound, like secrets shared,
Nature's voice, so pure and rare.

Beneath the boughs, where sunlight streams,
Dreams awaken, flutter like dreams.
Each whisper a tale of old,
In colors vibrant, green and gold.

Gentle breezes carry their song,
In harmony, where they belong.
Rustling softly, they dance and sway,
Nature's lullaby at the end of day.

And when the night begins to fall,
Silence reigns, yet hear them call.
In the stillness, their whispers weave,
A tapestry of life, to believe.

The Dance of the Wind

Through fields of gold, the wild winds roam,
Guiding the clouds, far from home.
They twist and twirl in a playful spree,
A ballet of freedom, wild and free.

Whirling softly through the trees,
Carrying laughter, a gentle breeze.
They beckon leaves to join the fun,
In this dance, under the sun.

From mountain tops to oceans wide,
They roam the world, with grace and pride.
A symphony crafted in whisper and rush,
In every moment, a thrilling hush.

And as the night starts to descend,
The wind hums low, as if to send
A message of calm, of peace within,
The dance continues, forever spin.

The Memory of a Snowflake

A flake descends from sky so bright,
Gliding down in soft moonlight.
Each pattern unique, a fleeting grace,
It kisses the earth, then leaves no trace.

Whispers of winter dance in the air,
Silence surrounds, as if in prayer.
Time slows down, a moment to hold,
In the chill, warmth quietly unfolds.

Children laugh, with cheeks aglow,
Building dreams in the soft, white snow.
A snowflake's tale, brief yet sublime,
Forever etched in the heart of time.

As sunlight beams, it melts away,
Yet memories linger in hearts that play.
For every flake like a fleeting jest,
Reminds us to cherish life's coldest quest.

Undercurrents of a Gentle Stream

Whispers of water weave through the stone,
A dance of reflections, softly grown.
Ripples that shimmer in dappled light,
Carry the secrets of day and night.

Beneath the surface, life ebbs and flows,
In the cool embrace, tranquility grows.
Fish dart swiftly, a flash in the deep,
Where shadows play, and the current keeps.

The trees lean down, their branches sway,
A symphony sung in a gentle way.
Leaves rustle softly, a sweet refrain,
In the hush of the woods, where peace shall reign.

Nature's heartbeat, a soothing song,
In every bend, where we all belong.
With each soft ripple, a timeless dream,
Carved by the whispers of a gentle stream.

Kisses of Morning Light

The sun peeks through the trees,
With whispers of the day,
Each light a gentle kiss,
Chasing the night away.

Dewdrops cling to soft blades,
Sparkling like tiny gems,
The world begins to wake,
As morning light condemns.

Birds chirp a sweet refrain,
In melodies so bright,
Nature sings in harmony,
Welcoming the light.

With each new ray of dawn,
Hope dances in the air,
Kisses of pure sunshine,
A moment rare and fair.

A Love Letter to the Horizon

Oh horizon, wide and free,
You hold my dreams in sight,
Your colors bleed and blend,
A canvas of pure light.

I gaze upon your endless line,
Where earth and sky embrace,
Each sunset whispers secrets,
In this sacred space.

Your beauty steals my breath,
With every shade you bring,
In twilight's warm embrace,
My heart begins to sing.

A love letter unwritten,
In hues of orange and gold,
Forever I will cherish,
The stories you unfold.

The Gift of a Morning Shower

Raindrops dance on rooftops bright,
Whispers of the dawn's soft light.
Nature wakes with gentle grace,
Life anew in every place.

Fragrant earth and blooms arise,
Kissing clouds and painted skies.
A symphony of freshened air,
Hope renewed, shedding despair.

Children laugh and puddles splash,
Joyful moments, memories flash.
Each droplet sings a tender song,
In this world where we belong.

As the sun begins to glow,
Nature's beauty starts to show.
In every shower, gifts await,
A dance of life that won't abate.

The Palette of Sunset Hues

As daylight fades, the canvas glows,
Streaks of orange, pinks, and shows.
The horizon kissed by evening flame,
A fleeting beauty, never the same.

Whispers of night in colors of gold,
Stories of old, quietly told.
In every shade a dream is spun,
A gentle reminder that day is done.

Clouds like dancers, twirling high,
Painting visions across the sky.
With each brushstroke, a tale to weave,
In the stillness, hearts believe.

As stars emerge, the colors blend,
A perfect moment that will not end.
In twilight's embrace, we find our rest,
In the palette of hues, we are blessed.

A Dialogue with the Dusk

The sun dips low, the sky ignites,
Whispers of day begin their flights.
Shadows grow, a soft embrace,
Night's veil falls, time slows its pace.

Stars awaken, twinkling bright,
They join the dance of fading light.
Owl calls out, its haunting tune,
A serenade to the rising moon.

Winds carry secrets, soft and sweet,
Footsteps hush on the evening street.
Conversations fade into twilight,
Dusk and I share our soft delight.

In this hour, all dreams unfold,
Stories of the night, untold.
With every sigh, the world exhales,
Dusk, our canvas, as stillness prevails.

The Hush of Falling Snow

Silent whispers touch the ground,
In a cloak of white, peace is found.
Each flake dances, a twirling grace,
Nature's soft hymn, a gentle embrace.

Branches bow under the weight,
A crystal world, a tranquil fate.
Footprints muffled, the world asleep,
In snowy dreams, secrets we keep.

The night is still, the air is clear,
A world transformed, winter's cheer.
Hearts unite in cozy glow,
Wrapped in warmth, we watch the snow.

As dawn approaches, a glimmered light,
Sparkles awaken, a pure delight.
In the silence, we share our thoughts,
In the hush of snow, love is caught.

Remnants of an Ancient Forest

In whispers soft, the trees still sway,
A memory of life in emerald play.
Beneath the boughs, the shadows creep,
Where silent secrets lie in sleep.

The roots entwined in earth's embrace,
Tell stories lost, time cannot trace.
Moss carpets the ground like a gentle sigh,
As birds of old sing a lullaby.

Ferns unfurl in morning's grace,
Holding time in their tender face.
A sacred bond with the skies above,
In every branch, a tale of love.

Yet storms may come and ages turn,
But in their hearts, the embers burn.
For in this realm of ancient lore,
The forest whispers forevermore.

The Radiance of First Light

As dawn breaks on the slumbering hills,
A golden hue the landscape fills.
The sun peeks out with gentle grace,
Painting the world in a warm embrace.

Birds awaken with songs so sweet,
A rhythm that makes the heart's pulse beat.
Each note a promise, each chirp a prayer,
In the crisp air, hope lingers there.

Dewdrops glisten on blades of green,
Reflecting the light—a vibrant sheen.
Nature stirs with a vibrant sigh,
As the day blooms under the sky.

The canvas brightens as shadows flee,
In every corner, life whispers free.
A fresh beginning, a moment to seize,
In the radiance of dawn's gentle breeze.

Moonlight on Quiet Waters

The moon hangs low, a silver thread,
It dances on waters, softly spread.
Whispers of night in gentle sway,
Stars join in, for the dreams at play.

Ripples of peace on the glassy tide,
Nature's secrets in the night abide.
A gentle breeze sings a lonesome tune,
While shadows embrace the light of the moon.

Reflections shimmer, a celestial show,
In quiet moments, the heart's aglow.
Silence wrapped in a cool embrace,
As time drifts slowly in this sacred space.

Under the sky where the wishes soar,
The night calls softly, forevermore.
In moonlight's glow, all worries cease,
A tranquil haven, a realm of peace.

The Silent Song of the Meadow

In fields where wildflowers softly sway,
A melody whispers at the close of day.
Beneath the sky, a canvas so wide,
Nature's own hymn, a gentle guide.

The grasses dance in the warm, soft air,
While butterflies flit without a care.
Every petal tells a story untold,
In shades of pink, yellow, and gold.

The sun dips low, casting shadows long,
As crickets emerge, to join the song.
A tapestry woven with silence and grace,
In the meadow's heart, a sacred place.

With every breeze, and each fleeting light,
The silent song brings the world to right.
In nature's arms, find solace and cheer,
In the meadow's embrace, all is clear.

Milton Keynes UK
Ingram Content Group UK Ltd.
UKHW021241191124
451300UK00007B/174